I love you,
Mama Noten

Our Inward Journey

Our Inward Journey

Written by Karen Ravn

Illustrated by Dona Aquaro Perry

Calligraphy by Rick Cusick

Hallmark Editions

Printed in the United States of America.
Standard Book Number: 87529-565-7

Our Inward Journey

Like you...
    I am a traveler
    in the world
    that lies around me.
    I journey on the roads
    of my experiences,
    my sensations
    and my interactions.

Like you...
    I belong
    to this outside world.
    I fit in it
    like one very tiny piece
    of a giant puzzle.

But like you...
    I know another world...
    a world that lies within me,
    that belongs to me.
    It is like a puzzle, too...
    made up of feelings
    and ideas and emotions...
    all mine
    to fit together as I choose.

    And even as I travel
    through the outside world,
    I'm always trying to keep in touch
    with who I am...
    always seeking out
    the wonders
    of the quiet world within me.

I am a questioner...
always wanting reasons,
needing to know why,
seeking the serenity
of certainty.

I am a questioner
grown used to solving puzzles...
expecting explanations,
then held spellbound by the unexplained,
the grand mysteries
of time, of space, of life itself.

I float among these secrets
like a swimmer
in a dark and silent river.
I reach into their shadowy depths
and come up empty handed.
I contemplate their vastness
and know a quiet sense of awe.

I am an individual...
    my own distinctive self
    with my own identity.
    I am like a snowflake
    that is different from all others,
    with abilities and talents,
    emotions and opinions,
    ideals and beliefs...
    all shaped into a pattern
    never seen before.

I am an individual,
sensing quiet pride
in my uniqueness.

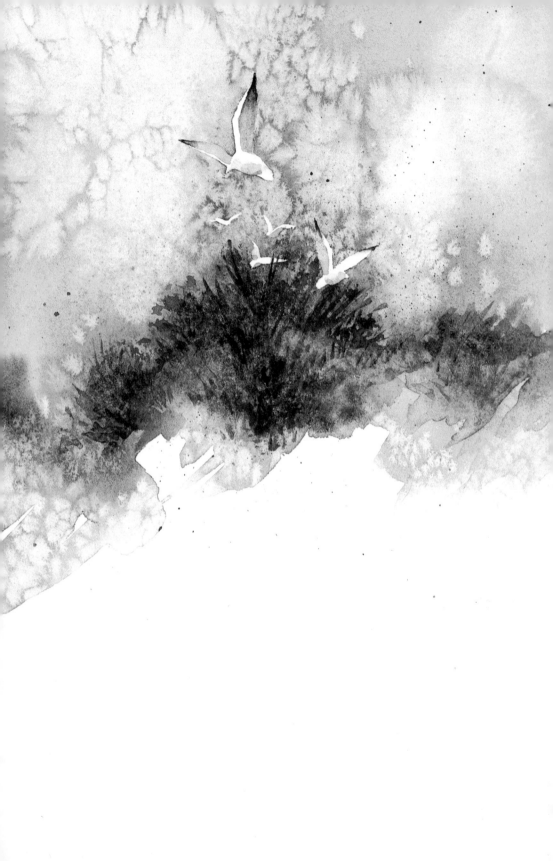

I am a friend...
    laughing, talking, needing,
    being needed.
    Mine is one note
    in a harmony
    of different tastes and likings...

    one voice
    in a chorus
    singing songs in unison
    that can't be sung alone...
    songs composed of fellowship,
    of trust
    and quiet closeness.

I am a child at play...
who dances like a buoyant kite
caught up by a mischievous breeze.
I dart and drift
and glide and soar.

Then I stop sometimes abruptly,
motionless a moment,
delighting in the heady atmosphere...
savoring the peaceful view
spread out before me
at these heights of freedom.

I am a collector...
of the multitude of sounds and colors,
tastes and smells and textures
here to treat my senses
every day.

I am a collector
of assorted facts and theories,
accomplishments and goals,
memories and mementoes.

I count these treasures
possessively,
like a contented monarch
cradling coins,
and I take a quiet satisfaction
in such splendid riches.

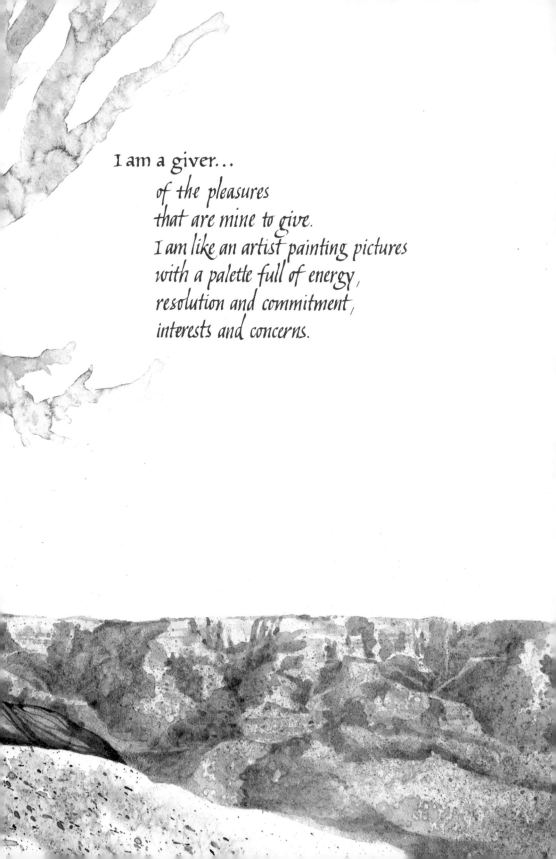

I am a giver...
    of the pleasures
    that are mine to give.
    I am like an artist painting pictures
    with a palette full of energy,
    resolution and commitment,
    interests and concerns.

If there is beauty in my offerings
for others,
there is beauty in them for me, too...
a special warmth of heart...
a lasting peace of mind.

I am a believer...
　　　accepting much on faith...
　　　taking much for granted.
　　　I trust my past experience
　　　as an animal
　　　trusts its instincts.

I don't doubt
that dawn will follow night,
that the sky will stretch
above my head,
that the earth will lie
beneath my feet.

For me there is a calm security
in knowing that some things
have always been,
that some things
will always be.

I am a loner...
    who enjoys solitude
    like a room
    kept to myself
    where I can set up my ideas
    like furniture to suit me
    and hang up all my fondest dreams
    like pictures on the walls.

    I only need to satisfy myself
    with the arrangements,
    and when I do
    I'm comfortable, relaxed,
    at perfect ease.

I am a doer...

    sometimes hesitant of purpose...
    wandering in deserts
    of pressure and frustration...
    confused by bright mirages
    of success.

And yet I am rewarded by those moments...
those refreshing, sweet oases
when I lose myself
in concentrated effort
and find the quiet meaning
of fulfillment.

I am a lover...
        sharing with another
        a tide of deepest feelings.
        I exchange a part of me
        for a part of someone else...
        like a wave that leaves its foam
        upon the shore,
        then carries polished grains of sand
        back with it out to sea.

        We are separate...
        as the ocean and the land,
        yet united, as they are,
        on a tranquil beach of understanding,
        tenderness and caring.

I am one of many...
  equal with my brothers and my sisters...
  conscious of our common past
  and future...
  encouraged by our common hopes
  and yearnings...
  strengthened by our common dedication.

  I feel a quiet comfort
  in our sameness
  as we make our way together...
  each on a separate path,
  yet all in the same direction.

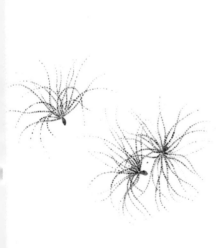

Like you…
I am a traveler
in the outside world.
Like you, I journey on the roads
of my experiences,
my sensations
and my interactions…

...always trying to keep in touch
with who I am ...
always seeking out
the faith and understanding,
the promise, the fulfillment
and the joy
that warm and beautify
the quiet world within me.

Printed on Hallmark Eggshell Bookpaper.
Designed by Rick Cusick and Dona Aquaro Perry.